Math Masters

Operations and Algebraic Thinking

HENRY FORD'S FANTASTIC FACTORY

Identify and Explain Patterns in Arithmetic

Lila Greene

PowerKiDS press™

NEW YORK

Published in 2015 by The Rosen Publishing Group, Inc.
29 East 21st Street, New York, NY 10010

Book Design: Katelyn Londino

Photo Credits: Cover (Henry Ford) UniversalImagesGroup/Getty Images; cover (Ford car plant) Archive Photos/
Hulton Archive/Getty Images; pp. 3–24 (metal texture) Phiseksit/Shutterstock.com; pp. 3–24 (metallic text background)
Color Symphony/Shutterstock.com; p. 5 Keystone Features/Hulton Archive/Getty Images; pp. 7, 17, 19 (car icon)
courtesy of Library of Congress; p. 9 Herbert Gehr/Time & Life Pictures/Getty Images; p. 11 Hulton Archive/Getty Images;
p. 13 (steering wheel icon) Car Culture/Car Culture ® Collection/Getty Images; p. 15 Keystone-France/Gamma-Keystone/
Getty Images; p. 19 (assembly line) Omikron -/Photo Researchers/Getty Images; p. 19 (tire icon) Peter Gudella/
Shutterstock.com; p. 21 Underwood Archives/Archive Photos/Getty Images; p. 22 Bloomberg/Getty Images.

Library of Congress Cataloging-in-Publication Data
Greene, Lila, 1984 - author.
 Henry Ford's fantastic factory: identify and explain patterns in arithmetic / Lila Greene.
    pages cm. — (Math masters. Operations and algebraic thinking)
 Includes index.
ISBN 978-1-4777-4941-8 (pbk.)
ISBN 978-1-4777-4942-5 (6-pack)
ISBN 978-1-4777-6413-8 (library binding)
1. Pattern perception—Juvenile literature. 2. Mathematics—Juvenile literature. 3. Assembly-line methods—Juvenile
literature. 4. Ford, Henry, 1863-1947—Juvenile literature. I. Title.
QA40.5.G74 2015
 513—dc23
                          2014004964

Manufactured in the United States of America

CPSIA Compliance Information: Batch #WS15RC: For further information contact Rosen Publishing, New York, New York at 1-800-237-9932.

CONTENTS

WHO WAS HENRY FORD?

Have you ever heard of Henry Ford? He was a famous American who lived in the late 1800s and early 1900s. He had ideas that changed the automobile **industry**.

Cars cost a lot of money when they were first invented, but Ford came up with ideas to make them affordable. He invented a car called the Model T. It was cheap to produce. That made it possible for many people to buy Model Ts.

Many people think of the Model T (left) as one of the most important cars in history. The smaller car is one of the first cars Ford ever made. He called it the Quadricycle. →

5

Before Ford invented the Model T, cars were made one at a time. Ford thought it would be cheaper to build cars using moving assembly lines. An assembly line is a manufacturing **process** where the work is divided into steps. A product on an assembly line moves past the workers. Each worker is trained to do just one step, such as making or attaching the same part to every car.

Moving assembly lines allow manufacturers to make goods more quickly. That's why their goods cost less.

Ford didn't invent the moving assembly line, but he perfected the process.

→

7

PATTERNS IN MATH

Each worker on the moving assembly line **repeated** the same task on every car. When processes repeat, they sometimes form patterns. A pattern is a form or order on which other things are based.

The different tasks at Ford's factory sometimes formed patterns. Whether it's how much of something the workers produced, or how fast they produced it, patterns can teach us a lot about math. Let's use examples from the Ford factory to learn about patterns in math.

Patterns often appear in addition and multiplication problems.

ONE STEP AT A TIME

Workers on the moving assembly line stayed in place while the cars passed in front of them. Each worker attached their part, and the car then moved on to the next worker. This continued until the job was done.

Imagine that a worker was in charge of attaching steering wheels to Model T cars. Every time they attached a steering wheel, the total number of steering wheels increased by 1. What happens when you add 1 to another number?

Use the number table on page 11 to answer this question. The table shows that every time you add 1 to a number, that number changes from odd to even, or from even to odd. Knowing this pattern can help you solve math problems.

Groups with an even number of objects can be split into 2 smaller, equal groups. Groups with an odd number of objects can't be broken into 2 equal groups. One group will have one more object than the other.

Adding even numbers always results in an even sum. Adding odd numbers always makes an even sum, too. Adding an even group and an odd group always results in an odd sum. You can use these patterns to make math easier.

Groups with an even number of objects are made up of pairs. Groups with an odd number of objects are made up of pairs with one extra object. Practice adding even and odd groups of steering wheels. Are the sums for these math problems even or odd?

→

odd

1 = ⊗

3 = ⊗ ⊗
⊗

5 = ⊗ ⊗
⊗ ⊗
⊗

even

2 = ⊗ ⊗

4 = ⊗ ⊗
⊗ ⊗

6 = ⊗ ⊗
⊗ ⊗
⊗ ⊗

even + even = even
2 + 2 = 4

⊗⊗ + ⊗⊗ = ⊗⊗
⊗⊗

odd + odd = even
5 + 3 = 8

⊗⊗ + ⊗⊗ = ⊗⊗
⊗⊗ ⊗ ⊗⊗
⊗ ⊗⊗
⊗⊗

even + odd = odd
4 + 1 = 5

⊗⊗ + ⊗ = ⊗⊗
⊗⊗ ⊗⊗
⊗

PRODUCING MORE

As time passed, the Ford factory produced cars more quickly. Imagine that over the course of a month, the factory produced more cars each week than it did the week before.

Imagine Ford's factory produced 1 car the first week, 4 cars the second week, 7 cars the third week, and 10 cars the fourth week. Do you notice a pattern in these numbers? Each number is 3 more than the previous number.

Notice that these numbers are changing from odd to even. If this pattern continues, how many cars would the factory make in the fifth week? Is that an odd or even number? →

1, 4, 7, 10, ____

Henry Ford worked on perfecting the moving assembly line for many years. At their peak, moving assembly lines cut production time almost in half. That meant the workers could make double the cars in the same amount of time.

When you double something, you multiply it by 2. Imagine the Ford factory doubled its production each week. If the workers built 2 cars the first week, how many did they produce each week for 5 weeks? Double the numbers to find out.

Any number multiplied by 2 is always even. So, all the numbers in a doubles pattern will be even.

→

week 1 ⟶ 2 cars
week 2 ⟶ 4 cars
week 3 ⟶ 8 cars
week 4 ⟶ 16 cars
week 5 ⟶ ?

MORE DOUBLING

If you double the amount of cars, you also must double the number of parts used to make them. All Model T cars had 4 wheels. The Ford factory produced 2 cars in the first week. Multiplying 2 times 4 equals 8, so they used 8 wheels.

The factory made 4 cars in the second week. Multiplying 4 cars by 4 wheels equals 16 wheels. Notice that 4 is the double of 2 and 16 is the double of 8. As you can see, doubling the **factors** in a multiplication equation causes the **product** to double, too.

You could multiply 4 x 2 or 2 x 4 and still get 8. It's the same with the number of tires in week 2. The order of factors doesn't matter in multiplication.

week 1
2 cars x 4 wheels = 8 wheels

week 2
4 cars x 4 wheels = 16 wheels

Imagine Ford sold 1 car a day. He would sell 1 car the first day, 2 cars by the second day, and 3 cars by the third day. If you continue this pattern, you'll see that any number times 1 is that same number.

What if Ford sold 5 cars a day? He would sell 5 cars on the first day, 10 by the second day, and 15 cars by the third day. Notice that **multiples** of 5 end in either 0 or 5. Now imagine that Ford sold 10 cars a day. What do you notice about multiplying a number by 10?

Multiples of 10 always end in 0. Why do you think some of the numbers on this table are in more than 1 column? →

number of days	1 car a day	5 cars a day	10 cars a day
1	1	5	10
2	2	10	20
3	3	15	30
4	4	20	40
5	5	25	50

A SUCCESSFUL COMPANY

Henry Ford's factory produced cars that everyone wanted to buy. Soon, his car company was the most famous in the world. People loved Ford's cars because they helped people travel to places they couldn't before.

Ford's company was successful because of its new production methods. Moving assembly lines allowed the workers to increase production in an organized way. Ford's company is still around today. Though production methods have changed, the company is still successful!

GLOSSARY

factor (FAK-tuhr) A number multiplied in a multiplication equation.

industry (IHN-duhs-tree) A group of companies that make the same goods.

multiple (MUHL-tuh-puhl) The number found by multiplying a number by another number.

process (PRAH-sehs) A series of steps.

product (PRAH-duhkt) The answer to a multiplication equation.

repeat (rih-PEET) To do the same thing many times.

INDEX